I0109199

SEASONS
OF
SUDDENLIES

McDougal & Associates
Servants of Christ and Stewards of the
Mysteries of God

SEASONS
OF
SUDDENLIES

AND OTHER REVELATIONS OF GOD'S TIMES AND SEASONS

BY

JERRY FITCH

DEDICATION

I dedicate this book to my beloved wife, Monique. Her love, patience, encouragement and understanding are the reason for the book. She has long encouraged me to write these current revelations in book form and share them with the world.

Monique is a woman of deep faith and great love. Although she's seldom in the spotlight, her presence is distinctly and divinely felt. She is my strength, my comfort, my encourager, my greatest fan and my love, and without her I would not become what I should be. So, Doll, I dedicate this book to you. Thank you for all you are to me, as well as to the God I serve.

ENDORSEMENT

Pastor Jerry Fitch is a good man. It is a pleasure for me to peruse his book and write this brief endorsement, first of the man and then of his work.

Pastor Jerry is an open book. What you see is what you get with him and his lovely wife, Monique. They are transparent and open before God and others. This is my most significant impression of them. How few people can earn this praise in the twenty-first century?

This book is straight from Jerry's heart. Here a loving pastor pours out his heart revelations for his sheep to graze upon. His revelations on Seed Plot and Seasons of Suddenlies alone are worth buying and reading the book. All the rest is a great big bonus.

I recommend both the man and his work for the Body of Christ.

Ronald E. Cottle, PhD, Ed.D
Founder, Christian Life School of Theology, Global Apostolic Council of Transformational Servant-Leaders

ENDORSEMENT

Season ... "A word that continues to be alive until it is manifested." Thank God we know God is always in control! He sets the times and seasons according to His will and plan.

Dr. Fitch shares much research as he encourages the reader to grasp the biblical truths of God's plan and faithfulness to bless His people in due season without fail. I especially appreciate the clever one-liners that grasp our understanding:

"GOD WILL DISPATCH SUDDENLIES FOR HIS CHILDREN!"

"BLESSINGS THAT CANNOT BE MANIPULATED BY MAN!"

"BEYOND EVERY ACT OF OBEDIENCE IS YOUR SUDDENLY!"

"The now word of Jesus to our lives and destiny!"

I highly recommend this book to anyone who needs an encouraging "now" word from God and the Scriptures as proof. As you read and study this work, I challenge you to expect the unexpected in *your* life.

James Adams
President, Anchor Bay Evangelistic Association
Founder, Alpha Christian College

ENDORSEMENT

Having Pastor Jerry Fitch as our spiritual Father has been vital to our personal lives as well as our ministry. As our spiritual father, he always makes himself available to us, even more so in a time of need. From the beginning of our ministry, we speak with him almost on a daily basis. He checks on the health of our church as well as our personal needs. His timing is great. I love how he calls out of the blue, but it's always at the perfect time.

Pastor Jerry makes himself available to me when I need guidance, advice or maybe just some encouragement. He has been more than a pastor to me; he's been a father figure to both my wife and myself.

Pastor Fitch and Monique (his wife and our spiritual Mom), play such an important role to my wife and me as our pastors. We are blessed to know that no matter what we face in ministry or life and that wherever the Fitches are at the moment, we have our loving and caring pastors praying and supporting us.

Each time the Fitches come to minister at The Freedom House, they make a deposit in the lives of our congregation. They are a blessing to the Body of Christ, to say the least, and we look forward with great anticipation to receiving from the Lord every time they come.

My wife, Jocelyn, and I are blessed to have them in our lives, and we have grown to love them more than words can say. We are honored to call Jerry and Monique Fitch our pastors, and I also know that we would not be where we are today in ministry without them.

Pastors Ernie and Jocelyn Hutchins
Founders and Senior Pastors
The Freedom House, Freeport and Brazoria, Texas
Founder, Ernie Hutchins Ministry

ENDORSEMENT

Jerry Joseph Fitch has been a friend of mine for the past forty-seven years. Through the years, we have become as close as (and even closer than) brothers. Having knowledge of each other as far back as 1970, we actually met in March of 1973 in a youth service at his home church, where I was preaching.

I remember the expectancy in my spirit as we drove up to that church. I could feel, as it were, the hand of God on my back, pressing me toward that service for some special reason. It was in that service, as I would later discover, that Jerry accepted the call of God on his life to preach the Gospel. I can still see him weeping under a heavy anointing as the Holy Spirit of God came upon him and set him apart for a dynamic ministry.

Dr. Fitch has labored intensely through the years in the pursuit of his education, as well as hands-on experience, for the sake of fulfilling the calling he knows God has placed upon him. He has traveled, preaching, pastored churches, pioneered works and coordinated conferences and ministerial campaigns, all in an effort to further the Kingdom of God and change lives for God's glory.

I am sure that in reading the words my friend has penned to paper, you will sense the passion for the Kingdom I have always seen in him through the years. His passion is effective, his labor is productive, and his efforts are constant, as he continues to do his part in building the Kingdom of God.

Dr. Fitch has been an inspiration to me through the years and continues to motivate God's good work in me, as all close friends in Kingdom ministry should. Be enriched as you partake of the giftings of God found in my brother in Christ.

My scripture verse to him is found in Philippians 1:3:

I thank my God upon every remembrance of you.

Rev. Jachin L. Dardar, Sr.
Prophetic Apostle
Founder and President,
Greater Harvest Ministries International

PERSONAL ENDORSEMENT

Although Jerry is my husband, he is also my pastor, my teacher and my very best friend. He is a family man, an awesome preacher, great pastor/evangelist and, above all, a fine Christian man. I am writing this about him from my perspective as his wife.

Because Jerry is my husband, I know and appreciate the sacrifices he has made, for me and so many others—too many to count. I thank God for my precious gift. I am fortunate to have such a wonderful husband.

Because Jerry is my pastor, I am not afraid to follow him as he leads me into a deeper revelation and walk with Christ. He is trustworthy in what he teaches. John 12:26 states, *"If any man serve me, let him follow me; and where I am there shall also my servant be: if any man serve me, him will my Father honour."*

Because Jerry is my teacher, I think of 1 Corinthians 13:4a (MSG), *"Love never gives what is lesser."* Through Jerry's example of God's relentless love, I have learned about loving others. Jerry loves our country, the United States of America, he loves Canada and the Canadian culture and people, and he has a deep love for the nation of Israel.

As my friend, Jerry is the most optimistic person I know. He will find good in any situation, and that is very refreshing. There is never a dull moment when I am with him. He adds so much joy to my life. I am very thankful to God for him!

First Corinthians 1:4-5 (NIV) says, *"I always thank God for you because of his grace given you in Christ Jesus. For in Him you have been enriched in every way, in all your speaking and in all your knowledge."*

The revelations my husband shares with you in this book are what are considered "now words." He walks in uncharted territory, as God has revealed Himself to us in this day in a new and dynamic way. Jerry dares to say what he senses God is speaking to him. Many ministers have spoken over Jerry that he walks in the revelations of God. One in particular, back in 1984, prophesied to Jerry that God had given Him revelations and that He had put healing in his hands. And it's true. Jerry's life and ministry have been committed to God, to live out the fullest of His will and to walk and speak His revelations. God uses him in healings and miracles, and yet that hasn't changed the fact that he sees himself as only a vessel that God can flow through.

The revelations in this book have changed our own lives, as we have walked out the understanding of them. This book will be a blessing and a life-changing word for all who read and apply the principles found in it. Enjoy my husband's book and, above all, be blessed in Christ!

Monique Fitch

CONTENTS

FOREWORD BY LEO CALVIN PRICE

An ancient rabbinical legend tells of a man named Simon who lived in Krakow, Poland. Simon had a vivid dream about a great treasure buried under a bridge in the city of Prague, many miles away. Being a poor man, the dream of the treasure excited him. When the dream reoccurred several times, Simon decided that he must go to Prague and search for the treasure.

When he reached Prague, Simon instinctively went directly to the bridge of his dreams. A sentry saw him probing around and demanded to know what he was doing. Simon told the sentry about his dreams and his long journey from Krakow. "You foolish man," the sentry replied, "don't you know you can't believe everything you dream? I have dreamed many times about a man named Simon who lived in Krakow. In the dream, there was a treasure buried under the stove in his kitchen. Should I, therefore, journey to Krakow in search of this treasure?" Whereupon, politely but firmly, the sentry told Simon to get out of town.

Simon returned to his house in Krakow, looked under the kitchen stove and, behold, there he found a great treasure, which enabled him to live comfortably for the rest of his life.

The ancient Rabbis always ended the story with these words, "The treasure was always in Krakow, but the knowledge of it was in Prague."

There were 3.3 billion Internet users as of November 30, 2015. Bill Clinton once said, "When I took office, only high energy physicists had ever heard of what is called the World Wide Web ... , now, even my cat has its own page." In just ONE minute on the Internet, Google performs two million searches.

You and I are also searching for something. Our hearts are empty and our heads are full.

We have knowledge and little understanding. We have passion and no purpose, which produces meaninglessness. We have purpose and no passion, which makes us powerless. Ours is a world in which people don't know what they want and are willing to go through Hell to get it. But God says, *"Ye shall seek me, and find me, when ye shall search for me with all your heart"* (Jeremiah 29:13).

This book will aid and guide you to the treasure. It is not a Band-aid to cover our wounds of mistakes, failures, sins and ineptness; it is a guide to help us secure our future.

For your longings there is fulfillment, and to your questions there are answers. Begin with God's Word, the Bible. Start there, and then pick up *Seasons of Suddenlies.* It's "due time."

Leo Calvin Price

FOREWORD BY DR. JERRY EDMON

I was especially intrigued with the manuscript that was given me on the *Seasons of Suddenlies*. Dr. Jerry Fitch brings God's Word into terms that are applicable to the challenges that we as believers face. *Seasons of Suddenlies* is a look into the tendencies and nature of our heavenly Father and truly brings to light His ability and desire to transform our ashes into beauty and our darkness into light.

Providence, in the sense that God has all the numbers lined up to make things happen ... it's deeper than that. Rather, it is a matter of His love that brings us into His purpose from one season to another, and even the times of adversity that seem so difficult are actually doing a work in us that brings us to another place in His purpose.

Seasons are an indication of a design and the one thing God wants from us is, many times, the thing we have most difficulty giving Him—our trust. Our trust and obedience are the gateway to the "suddenlies" that God has for us.

As Jerry says, "He changes the seasons and guides history." The *Season of Suddenlies* are governed by the hand of our loving heavenly Father. On that hope we are anchored.

Dr. Jerry Edmon
Senior Pastor, Family Worship Center
Elgin, Texas

INTRODUCTION

One year, during a trek back to Louisiana for our annual family reunion, as my wife and I were traveling, the Lord spoke to my heart and began dealing with me about "seasons." For the next four hours, as we journeyed to our destination, I sensed the Lord dictating to me the concept of seasons and what He had begun to do within His Body (the Church). I listened intently as He spoke definitively about certain seasons that the Church had entered into without fully recognizing the times (see Luke 19:44).

Over the course of the next few years and even to this day, God continues to enlighten me about His seasons and their relevance to us today as a Church. His Word continues to grow within my spirit as I pursue and follow

His directives about this time in which we have been allowed to navigate into His eternal purposes. I have no reservations about telling you that God has given me "revelation knowledge" about these times. I also have no reservations that as a student of His Word, I support what He has spoken to me with that Word, which is the final authority.

As a young minister, I made a determination in my life that I would speak what God gave me. I made a choice to become a student of His Word and to *"rightly [divide] the word of truth."* I studied and researched for myself, but I also sat under great men of God who had paved the way for me to embark on the "next season of the Lord." I can say that I had and have a good foundation that these men laid out *for* me and *in* me.

I discovered at a young age a scripture that has, for the most part, defined my purpose as a preacher of God's Word and a minister to His people. Isaiah 50:4-7 speaks of Jesus' preparation for ministry and His difficulties, as well as His determination to fulfill His call to humanity. I didn't know all this at the time of discovery, yet the scripture became a bulwark in my life. Later I would learn, as I studied the scripture, what exactly it meant.

I make no pretense about anything. I have no one to impress but God and Him alone. Yet I still realize that I must grow in favor, not only with God, but with man as well, just as Jesus did (see Luke 2:52). So I decided to educate myself in the Spirit, the Scriptures and in parochial schooling. I sought *the tongue of the learned* in order to be an encourager. I resisted the temptations to follow the ways of others in order to wholly follow Jesus. I set my face like a flint and knew that I would never be ashamed.

Have I always lived up to what I purposed by God's Word? Sadly, for me, no. But I've always been able to return, pick up from where I failed and continue the course God set for me.

In high school, I played football and learned that the running back may get tackled, but he must learn to always fall forward. I have learned that failure or falling is not final in the Kingdom of God, and I've learned to go forward and trust Him. Because of that, I have never turned my back on God.

Another scripture that has been my guide in ministry is found in Matthew 13:52. I realized through the years that somehow I have remained current without violating the Scriptures. God has given me revelation knowledge throughout my ministry, and the treasures I've been able to minister come, not only from old revelations, but also from new revelations. Both are necessary if we are to speak truth that will prevail and inevitably accomplish what the Word is designed to do.

This is the definition of what Jesus meant when He said, *"Ye shall know the truth, and the truth shall make* [not set, but make] *you free"* (John 8:32). What I have come to realize within the last few years is that God has called me and He has called you for seasons.

Isaiah 50:4 says that we are to speak a word *"in season"* in order to bring help to the weary. The word *season* in this text is the Hebrew verb *ut,* meaning "to sustain help, speak in season."

The tongue of the learned is to speak a sustaining word, a word that helps, in a particular season.

Throughout the course of this writing, we will discover the "seasons" of the Lord and develop an understanding of the most wonderful day humanity has ever experienced. In this great season of the Lord, get ready for the ride of your life!

Jerry Fitch
New Iberia, Louisiana

Chapter 1

A SEASON OF SUDDENLIES

"Though no one can go back and make a brand new start, anyone can start from now and make a brand new ending."

— Unknown

The Church age has been filled with seasons. From before the Reformation and beyond, to the great healing revivals and prophetic movements, to and through the Charismatic Movement, to this very time, we have experienced seasons. We are all familiar with the seasonal cycles of the planet, but I'm speaking about seasons that are not determined by the rotation of the Earth on its axis, but seasons determined by God Himself.

"While the earth remains,
Seedtime and harvest,
Cold and heat,
Winter and summer,
And day and night
Shall not cease."   Genesis 8:22, NKJV

Rest assured that the seasons of God will continue.

I tend to believe there is a deeper application to this scripture than we have understood. For example, we understand the twenty-four-hour period called a "day." But what about the phrase *"one day is with the Lord as a thousand years, and a thousand years as one day"* (2 Peter 3:8). We understand grammatically that this is a simile, but do we dare venture into uncharted waters to define it as we read it? Also, what about the times the phrase *"the Day of the Lord"* is used? Does it speak of a twenty-four-hour period or does it speak of an extended time period—perhaps a season?

It seems to me that God gives us vision and revelation in an embryonic form and, then, like an egg, it develops and grows with time. Of course it takes more than time for an egg to hatch. It first takes the fertilization process, then the laying of the fertilized egg. Following that it takes twenty-one days of the hen sitting on the egg providing adequate heat to develop the potential chick within. Of course there are more in-depth stages of growth within the egg, but for the most part, the egg is fertilized, laid and the hen sits on the egg, and the chick comes in time.

Our "fertilization" process is when the word comes to us in our spirit!

God "seeds" us with His Word and we become impregnated with His Word spoken to us. Following the seeding, we must provide adequate nourishment to the seed in order for it to grow within us. At this point, the seed is viable, although not yet visible. What makes it viable is the planting, and until the planting takes place, it will only remain as a seed, a potential harvest.

Once the seed becomes visible, there is the acknowledgement of the potential to produce a harvest. It is at this point that what has been viable and now is visible, becomes vital.

By definition, it exists as a manifestation of life! What once was viable but not yet visible now becomes visible then vital and now becomes valuable! As the seed grows, we begin to see formed within us the Word of the Lord.

It's not long before God begins to confirm His Word with signs and wonders which becomes to us an encouragement that we have definitely heard from God. And now the word which first came in embryonic form, seeded by God, developed within, becomes the substance from which we live and breathe and have our being. But it just didn't happen overnight; it took a season. In this case, a season can be defined as "a range or degree to which something extends."

God spoke to my spirit and said that we are to expect, in this season, some suddenlies. God speaks to us words in season, as much if not more than *chronos* (time as we understand; watch, day, year etc). When you have received a spoken word from the Lord and it may not have happened as of yet, but that does not mean it will not take place. It was spoken for a season and is a seasonal word that continues to be alive until it is manifested. Hear this: God adds to our yesterdays and enlarges our promises until the word is brought to completion.

But according to the original Greek, the definition of *chronos* denotes "a space of time, whether long or short." Its implication denotes duration whether long or short. According to *Vines Expository Dictionary of New Testament Words* by W. E. Vine, broadly speaking *chronos* expresses the duration of a period, while *kairos* stresses it as "marked by certain features." Thus, in Acts 1:7, *"the Father has set within His own authority"* both the times (*chronos*), the lengths of the periods, and the seasons (*kairos*), epochs characterized by certain events. May I say that if you have not begun to enjoy the quality that is ours as His children, it is past time for you to enter your season.

In Malachi 3:1, the writer declares that God *"will send [His] messenger, and he will prepare the way before [Him]: and the LORD, whom you seek, shall suddenly come to his temple, even the messenger of the covenant, whom you delight in."*

But, before we begin our discussion of the suddenlies, let us examine a few scriptures in order to understand the significance of appointed seasons and their possible relation to the suddenlies in our lives.

First of all, look at Numbers 9:2-3, 7 and 13. There is a recurring phrase in each of these verses—*"appointed season."* The phrase *"appointed season"* is from the Hebrew word *moed,* and it means "a designated season, an appointed time, a meeting." It speaks of feasts, appointed signs and assemblies. In Numbers, the particular season that is spoken about is the Passover. The Passover is one of seven Jewish feasts and, in particular, one of the three feasts required of the Jewish people to keep before the Lord yearly. The Passover is linked directly with deliverance of the children of Israel from Egypt. Under the better covenant, the Passover is also linked directly to us by Jesus being our Passover Lamb (see Hebrews 8:6). His blood was shed for our deliverance from sin, sickness and poverty and despair. I believe the feasts are not only practiced (historically) but hold a specific prophetic significance as well. They are defined by the Hebrew word *chad* meaning "a happy occasion."

When we speak of appointed seasons, the bottom line is that God is in control!

God sets and determines the times and the seasons according to His will. We do not control the seasons; we make adjustments to enjoy them. I remember, while pastoring in Michigan for seven years, that the natural seasons there were very distinct and very enjoyable for me. Spring maintained a briskness of the winter's past, while summer was as enjoyable as any place on earth I had experienced.

Fall is a beautiful time in Michigan, as the foliage changes colors making Michigan nothing short of a canvas of natural beauty. I am beginning to understand David, as he penned in Psalm 8:3-4, "*When I consider thy heavens, the work of thy fingers, the moon and the stars, which thou hast ordained; what is man, that thou art mindful of him?*" The psalmist marveled at God's majestic creation; he stood in awe at the beauty of a creation that truly only a Vreator could have painted! Tours are taken yearly for others to enjoy the handiwork that only God could paint!

Then comes winter! I personally did not have any problem enjoying the winter months in Michigan. In fact, I looked forward to winter and still do—although I now pastor in sunny Louisiana. While in Michigan, I remember that each year, as the cold, snow and ice would settle in, I would see signs popping up in yards, businesses and other locations that read: "THINK SPRING!"

I was in a winter wonderland, enjoying a season I had never experienced to this extent, and yet some were so tired of this season that they would seemingly protest against it. I get a little chuckle out of that; the people were so tired of the long, drawn-out winters that they would actually "root" for spring to arrive! I now understand how they felt because here in "sunny Louisiana" it's really hot! (I'm thinking about making a sign that reads "THINK WINTER!").

In Daniel 2:21, I believe there is an understanding we should all glean. *Gills Exposition of the Entire Bible* states it like this: "Day and night, summer and winter, times and seasons of prosperity and adversity ..." *The Message* Bible says, *"He changes the seasons and guides history .. ."* As I studied these two interpretations of this verse, I had to conclude that seasons (natural and supernatural) are not under the control of man, and they certainly do not happen by chance. They are governed by a supreme God, who is in charge of them and has the power to change them when He chooses. God changes the seasons.

God is not confined by time and space as we are. He is not restricted to a vacuum.

He transcends it all. He moves in and out of time and space and freely operates by His power. Regardless of what many may say, the earth is still the Lord's! He still rules all, and, when He chooses, He may overrule all by His providence.

As God changes our seasons, His divine intervention touches our destiny! You may have been in a time of adversity, but God moved into the sphere of your existence and determined that your destiny was not adversity but that of privilege! Poverty may fill your life, and you may have decided that this is your "lot" in life. But I want you to know that God is the One who changes seasons, and He can change your poverty to prosperity, your sin into salvation, your bondage to breakthrough, and your desire to destiny!

The Spirit of the Lord deposited a thought in my mind about the seasons of suddenlies. We've examined appointed seasons. Now we'll take a closer look at particular seasons, beginning with the season of suddenlies.

Expect the unexpected!

Suddenlies is defined as an unexpected occurrence; all of a sudden; at once. Have you ever considered what an unexpected occurrence is? It is something that happens when you didn't expect it to happen. God spoke to my heart and told me to "expect the unexpected" in this season of suddenlies!

So many of God's children live within the realm of the knowledge of upcoming blessings and not in the realm of the Suddenlies. We know when our paychecks come; we know when our Social Security payments come; we know when our Christmas bonus comes, when our vacation pay comes, etc. These are all good and there's not a thing wrong with these expected benefits; but what about living within the dimension of suddenlies when something unexpected takes place?

Let's add to the realm of the upcoming blessings by living within the realm of the unexpected blessings. We have entered the season when we can expect the unexpected! We have just crossed into the beginning of the season of suddenlies, and I believe God is going to dispatch Suddenlies for His children! I'm talking about blessings that cannot be manipulated by man and no one could have done this for you but God Himself!

Not everyone will experience suddenlies in their lives. Some churches are as blessed as they are ever going to be. They have entered into the maintain mentality and the survival mode. Sadly, some Christians and some entire church groups are as blessed as they're ever going to be. Some will not experience suddenlies because of doubt and unbelief, others because of belief systems that box God into a particular perimeter that says "God doesn't work that way." Still others may not experience suddenlies because of the traditions of men. They only reflect past seasons and refuse to go beyond what they know and enter into the realm of the unknown. Regardless of the reason many will not enjoy the suddenlies of

God, it is really tragic. I believe the "maintain mentality" represents small-minded people. It is a fear tactic that employs being boxed into a corner and being too fearful to move out in faith to trust an omnipotent God and its cousin is "survival mode."

Aristotle once said, "Fear is the pain of an anticipated evil!"

People actually defend an outcome that may never happen! They go through the emotional upheaval and suffer intensely in advance about something that may never transpire! Again, it's called the survival mode. I have heard it said that the decisions you make will define you or destroy you. I want to make right decisions, what about you?

Pentecost stands as a vivid reminder of many who refused to enter the season of suddenlies. According to Paul's writings to the church at Corinth, Jesus was seen once by more than five hundred people. For the sake of simplifying the math, let's use five hundred. Of the five hundred, only one hundred and twenty obeyed Jesus and went to Jerusalem to await the promise of the Holy Spirit. On that day, one hundred and twenty recipients were filled with the Holy Spirit and were infused with a power that had been released within them that would turn the world around! Three hundred and eighty people missed out on the greatest outpouring of their day by not being where God told them to gather. If there's a tragedy regarding Pentecost, here it is: three hundred and eighty people missed out on Jesus' prophetic word concerning the introduction of the Holy Spirit on planet Earth.

Beloved, do not be numbered among those that miss out on the greatest time of this earth's existence by not entering into the present season of God. To each season, there's a blessing and a tragedy. I choose the blessing, what about you?

Look at what transpired on the Day of Pentecost in Acts 2:1-2. One translation of verse 1 reads, *"As the day dawned..."* I like that.

A Season of Suddenlies

It is speaking of a new day, a new season, if
you will. This has never happened before. The
hundred and twenty were in Jerusalem out
of obedience to the risen Christ, as well as to
commemorate a festival. They were told to go
and wait for the promise of the Father. I submit
to you that they did not know what they were
waiting for or what to look for because the arrival of the Holy Ghost had not been defined or
outlined in a particular way or identified except
as He being the Comforter. They didn't know
what the Holy Spirit looked like and certainly
didn't expect what they got! But a new day
(season) was about to dawn. The church was
about to embark upon a new season that would
catapult her into the destiny designed for her
from before the beginning of time.

Verse 2 begins with the words, *"and suddenly."*
Look at that, an unexpected occurrence. All of
a sudden, at once, He, the Holy Spirit, arrived
on the scene as prophesied, and the season began that day and continues to this day!

This is proof positive that seasons have different lengths of duration. As defined, a *season*

indicates "an indefinite period of time, a period of time approximately twenty-four hours to longer periods (years)." And it all began because a few were willing to be obedient to the Word of God. Listen, God spoke to my spirit and said, "Beyond every act of obedience is your suddenly." I think that this is awesome. As we obey God, we can expect the unexpected.

Beyond every act of obedience is your suddenly!

We need to come to a place in our lives where there is an expectancy of God doing the unexpected. You may question, "What is the unexpected I should expect?" I cannot answer that for you, but I can say it is beyond what you know or think.

I am reminded of Ephesians 3:20, where Paul spoke to the church at Ephesus and declared: *"God is able to do exceeding abundantly above all that we ask or think according to the power that works in us..." The New Testament in Modern*

Speech (Richard Francis Weymouth) describes *exceedingly abundantly* as *"He who is able to do infinitely beyond all our highest prayers or thoughts."* According to that verse, we cannot even think of all that God can do for us, and its fulfillment is according to a power at work in us.

Let your imagination release your imprisoned possibilities. — Jerry Fitch

---

Listen, let your imagination release your imprisoned possibilities! The *"power at work within us"* is translated by *The Emphasized New Testament: A New Translation* (J.B. Rotherham) as *"the power which doth energize itself with us."* Think about that. What is it that you want God to do for you? He can do more!

I believe that the power that is at work in our lives is the Spirit of the living God working in us by faith. Release that power in your life and watch God do the unexpected. Trust in His ability to go beyond your needs, desires and wants, and allow Him to supernaturally manifest His greatness to you. He, the Holy Spirit, energizes Himself for us!

God has an unlimited resource that has been virtually untapped by His children, and He stands willing and able to give you His abundance, an abundance you don't have the ability to even think about it. What an awesome God we serve!

Acts 14:17 declares, *"God left not Himself without witness, in that He did good, gave us rain and fruitful seasons."* God will never be without proof on this earth. This is the day of fruitful seasons; enter in and be one who displays the graciousness of our Lord to a waiting world!

Chapter 2

A DUE SEASON

"If you can't explain it simply, you don't understand it well enough."

— Albert Einstein

Galatians 6:9 is a scripture that we've enjoyed over the years. It was spoken by Paul to the church of Galatia:

And let us not be weary [to give in to evil, to lose heart, and become a coward] in well doing: for in due season [in its own season] we shall reap if we faint not.

The definitions in parenthesis are from *A Linguistic Key To The Greek New Testament.*

The Greek word translated *due* is *idios,* and its implication also speaks of "harvest time." It is "an appointed time for reaping." *Fainting* means "to be exhausted as a result of giving in to evil." As you consider the application of this scripture, you'll find a couple of thoughts worthy of our consideration. First of all, doing good can wear you out! And yet doing good is directly linked with our harvest.

I would think that doing good as a Christian is automatic, and to some degree, it is. But here the Word says for us not to give in to evil and lose heart in doing good.

Secondly, I would submit, at this point, that it is our "lack" of realizing the harvest that we expect that would cause us to lose heart while doing good. Some may disagree with me on this point, but I tend to believe that, as we have been promised, that we reap what we sow, and we continue to sow good, and yet it seems like we are reaping the opposite, we can grow weary. We must remember that every season has a harvest time. We cannot faint or become weary in the journey. There's a due season coming.

According to the definition of *due* in this verse, there is in our future, our very own private season of reaping. I like how it is stated in *The New Testament in Modern English by* J. B. Phillips, *"Let us not grow tired of doing good, for, unless we throw in our hand, the ultimate harvest is assured."* The *Expanded Greek* by Kenneth S. Wuest says it like this, *"Let us not slacken our exertions by reason of the weariness that comes with prolonged effort in habitually doing that which is good. For in a season which in its character is appropriate, we shall reap if we do not become enfeebled through exhaustion and faint."* You see, it's not the doing good that causes us to faint; it's the waiting for the harvest. Knowing there's a harvest coming, let this be an encouragement to overcome any and every obstacle of discouragement that comes your way.

Many writers have labeled the book of Galatians as the "*Magna Carta* of the Church," in that it deals with the favor of Christian liberty in its defense against the teachings of the

Judaizers. The Judaizers wanted the Galatians to revert back to Judaism and follow the Law. Paul adamantly stood against their teachings and reminded the Galatians that what they had received by God came from "the hearing of faith." He also told them that they which had begun in the Spirit could not be "perfected by the flesh (the Law)."

We want to examine and define the use of the phrase *due season* in this chapter. In the scriptures we'll use, the phrase *due seasons,* as translated from the Hebrew, is always used without fail to mean "an appointed time, the unit of time of various lengths, His spoken Word, one's own private time, manner, specification, a designated appointment." Although we'll use different variations of the word, its meaning remains the same. Understanding how God views a *due season* will cause us to know His will for our lives and the seasons of our lives that will accompany our destiny.

In each due season, there will

always be specific blessings to accompany the times!

It is always important to know that the seasons overlap each other. In other words, when you've been in one season, another season will present itself and then another, and so forth. Understand that one season does not disqualify the last season, but embraces and enhances it to a greater fruition with the present season.

Have you ever received a notice that stated, "Past Due?" It simply meant that the remuneration for a deed done, a loan given, was past time for the agreement made between parties to be fulfilled. It is now up to the party with the outstanding "Past Due" notice to fulfill his part of the contract.

This notice is defined as "a specification or manner." When the specific manner of remuneration is not followed according to the agreement, there is what is called a "breach of contract or agreement." A breach of contract can bring serious consequences if not imme-diately rectified. It may have been an oversight on your part, but notice that it doesn't matter. What matters is that you are past due. This was the situation David addressed to the "chief of the fathers" when they first attempted to bring the Ark of the Covenant back to Jerusalem and failed. In 1 Chronicles 15:13, the same word *due*, *mispat* in the Hebrew, means "specifica-tion, manner" and is used to explain the terms of the contract and the consequences for failing to follow the terms.

Please understand, it is never God who is past due with His seasons; it is we who are late en-tering into the season He has appointed for us. The breach is not on God's part; it's on our part!

God's Word cannot be broken and He can never deny Himself; neither is He a man that He should lie. Therefore, we must be keenly aware of the seasons of the Lord and listen intently to His prophets, as He will not do any-thing without first revealing His will, so that His people may follow and enjoy the blessings of the season.

A Due Season

As I said in the introduction, God spoke to my heart on the way back to Louisiana about the seasons of the church. His Word was that the church was on the brink of the greatest times she has ever experienced. He spoke to me to let the church know that a now season has entered the church. Now it was time for the church to enter into the season!

Another Hebrew word defined *due seasons* is *et*, meaning "a unit of time of various lengths." Take a look at Leviticus 26:4, where God promises that He'll give rain in due season, and the land shall yield her increase, and the trees of the field shall yield their fruit.

The length of time your season will last depends upon your sowing!

May I say to you that the length of time your season will last depends upon your sowing! How often do you sow into God's Kingdom? And just as important, are you sowing in good ground? God rains upon our sowing in order to bring forth our harvest. The season of Him raining upon many of you is right now! You have sown, and now you are about to reap!

When we reap, it doesn't mean that it's time to stop sowing. The reaping is an encouragement to multiply our sowing because of our reaping.

I remember, in times past, when we'd sit in church and sing a chorus, "We need the rain Lord, we need the rain; we need the latter rain." Some of you may remember that chorus (now we're telling on age). We not only sang it; we got excited about it, and rightfully so. But we sang the chorus with the expectation of Jesus' coming to rapture us out of this planet. But the rain He's talking about is a season that will bring our sowing to fruition!

He's raining upon those seed prayers!

We have prayed about our lost loved ones, and He's raining upon those prayers. We've prayed about being able to do His perfect will and He's raining upon those seed prayers. (Oh, I like that, "seed prayers".) And what about all those other things that you've prayed about over time? Look for the rain because God's about to give you your harvest! Plant those seed prayers in your seed plot, and God will water with His rain, and we will reap a bountiful harvest.

Another use of the word *et* is found in Proverbs 15:23, where it speaks of a *"word spoken in due season is good." Due season* here is also defined as "His Word spoken." It speaks of a rhema word or the spoken word of God. Have we really ever come to realize the power of God's spoken word? Have we ever come to realize the power of you and I speaking what He speaks?

Many years ago the church entered into a season of speaking God's Word. Many attacked the teaching, and others embraced it. Great things transpired within that season, but soon it waned. Although many refused to let go of the teaching, and rightly so, still the season seemed to fade away. I sense that God is restoring that season again, but with greater emphasis than before. I want to say to you that when we receive a prophetic word from God and speak that word, God has already aligned Heaven in order for that word to be fulfilled. The power of His creative Word takes what is not and makes something out of nothing! His spoken word is His platform to accomplish His purposes. It calls into being what has not existed before and creates a course for His Word to come to pass.

Hear what I'm about to say: God is taking this somewhere; He's just not speaking to hear Himself talk.

You and I are the destination of His Word!

Remember the "now word" of Jesus to your life and destiny (future). God doesn't give you a past word. His Word is in your future, awaiting your arrival! It's time to make a break with your past and make a break for your future! But remember that the Word given is in embryonic form and is growing and enlarging and multiplying as it awaits your arrival!

Our circumstances do not define us or our destiny; His spoken word does!

Whenever a spoken word is declared into your life, believe it and receive it. Believe the Word of the Lord. Believe His prophetic spoken word in your life and receive it, even though there may be nothing in your life that seems to substantiate it. The spoken word is a living word, and it sets into motion an action to change your circumstances and your life. I discuss more of this in the final chapter of the book.

Moed is another Hebrew word used to define *due season,* and it means "an appointed time, designated time, meeting and season." It speaks of feast times, appointed sign, and assemblies. Do you know that the same way you can break an appointment with your doctor, you can break your appointment with your God-given destiny? Consider this, it's not God's will that any would perish but all come to life, and yet so many perish without God and are eternally separated from Him. They broke their appointment with their destiny. God's design for your life includes a designated appointment with His seasons of blessings for you.

The phrase *due season* also means "an indefinite period of time, an event, occurrence." In the Greek, specifically in Galatians 6:9, the phrase *due season* is translated from the word *kairos*, meaning "an opportune time, proper time, due time." It also speaks directly to the harvest. God provides for us seasons of opportunity, *kairos* if you will, to enter into His design for our lives. I strongly believe that there are seeds of destiny deposited in our lives before birth.

At the point where you discover your destiny, you will move

positively into your "discovery zone" and cease to make decisions based upon your circumstance!

You must take powerful, forward steps in faith believing, knowing that you have His direction. Set your face like a flint and don't be delayed! I've heard it said, "Seize the opportunity of a lifetime within the lifetime of that opportunity" We have found over the years that windows open and windows close. Seize the opportunity to embrace all God has for you in the season of open windows.

How many of you reading this have gotten a word from the Lord, you knew it came from God and you believed the promise, and yet, instead of you walking in the realm of abundance, immediately the enemy was dispatched from Hell to steal from you everything God said He was going to give to your life? You may even have reached an impasse in life and question the availability of God. You may have faced confrontations in your life when you felt you were face to face, eyeball to eyeball with the enemy. But God's Word says that the Greater One lives within you. You may wrestle the enemy, but you'll be on top, and when the bell rings and the last round is over, it's going to be you who is victorious over all the power of the enemy!

You may have been knocked down, but you haven't been knocked out! The enemy may have knocked your breath out, but there's a second wind of the Spirit of the Living God with the breath of a prophetic spoken word that is arising in your heart and you'll do what God said you can do and accomplish all He has determined for you do!

That, my friend, is the power of the spoken word! And this is the season to arise and become all He has created you to be. Do not get discouraged or disillusioned. The Lord spoke to my heart and said, "The strength of the weapon the enemy has chosen to use against you is an indication of the significance of the harvest God has in your future!" This is your season!

Declare it: THIS IS MY SEASON!

The strength of the weapon the enemy has chosen to use against you is an indication of the significance of the harvest God has in your future!

Chapter 3

A Season of Turnaround

(Expect The Unexpected)

"Destiny is not a matter of chance, it's a matter of choice; it's not a thing to be waited for, it's a thing to achieve."
— William Jennings Bryan

Another season that God has ordained we enter into is the season of turnaround. It seems to me that God wants to break the cycle of us doing good, experiencing great things, then having an unexplainable reversal to the same-old same-old.

While driving into Florida on March 23, 2015 at dusk, I received a literal sign from the Lord. There was a lighted, flashing road sign, a billboard, if you will, that read; EXPECT THE UNEXPECTED! When I saw that, excitement hit my spirit in a new and living way. Here was what God had been speaking to my heart for a couple of years now, and He put a sign out there just for me! It caused me to rehearse the prophetic word that was given to me years earlier. The timing of prophetic words given speaks more to seasons, as opposed to our calendar year. Prophetic words will continue over the course of time, even several years, and intensify with time.

One week after I saw that sign, I drove to Alabama and when I was coming back into Florida, I looked for the sign, and it was gone! I thought to myself, "The Florida DOTD (Department of Transportation and Development) does not put up a lighted, flashing sign for only a week (and it could have been less for all I know) and then take it down." I went been back and forth to and from

Louisiana a number of times since that visitation (for my part, I take it to be no less than a visitation from God), and the sign is nowhere to be found. I have no reservations in telling the world that God put that sign up just for me! I had been in prayer for years about the seasons and the revelations that I had received. The promises He had given to me were watered by agreement with His Word. His promises took precedence over my life since the inception of the seed of suddenlies (unexpected occurrences). I knew the word He had given me was prophetic, and I have ministered that word at a number of churches. I know that I have gotten a word from the Lord! I have never doubted it before, and I certainly have no reason to believe otherwise.

"It's not what you look at that matters. It's what you see!" — David Thoreau

---

I saw God telling me to EXPECT THE UNEXPECTED!

EXPECT THE UNEXPECTED. This word fills every fiber of my being. I awaken in the morning with it ringing in my spirit. I claim it throughout every day of my life. I declare it, that it's personal, it's my word from my Father! I have never been one to look for confirmations of God's Word. I mean, who can confirm God? But I must confess that I have rejoiced over and again for this confirmation of God by God Himself! I had said, in my youthful indiscretion as a minister, "I don't need a sign." I said that because I had no doubt that God would do exactly what He said He would do. It wasn't because I was cocky or boastful. I just completely trusted God. I still trust Him completely, but I soon realized that God wanted to confirm His Word with signs following.

God's Word declares that signs "*follow* [accompany, to follow along side] *them that believe*" (Mark 16:17). I didn't want to be part of a perverse generation that seeks signs, but I also do not want to be a part of those who dispel the very nature and work of God through signs. Therefore, I welcome His signs—whether they are prophetic, healings, salvations or lighted flashing road signs. Whatever arena His signs enter, I welcome them.

God has a personal sign for you!

One of the definitions of the Hebrew word *mood* (*season*) is "an appointed sign." According to this definition, God has a personal sign for you. God's design for your life includes a designated appointment with His season of blessings for you.

The Greek word *idios* (*season*) in Galatians 6:9 means "one's own, private sign," your own sign. According to this definition, there is in your future your very own private sign in this season of reaping. (*For in due season, you shall reap if you do not faint.*)

I'm speaking to you by the revelation of the Lord to expect the unexpected to fill your life. God has your own personal, prophetic word that fits you perfectly, and, by faith in His Word, you move into His dimension of the unexpected! God gave me my own private sign that evening as I entered into Florida. But that word wasn't only for me; it was for the Church as a whole.

When He first began speaking to me about suddenlies and seasons, it was a word spoken to the Church. Over time, it has become personal for me, as well as corporate.

I am saying to you by the Spirit of the Lord, EXPECT THE UNEXPECTED!

TURNAROUND

There are a number of areas where we need a turnaround. As we discuss a few, expect the unexpected during this season to become the norm and not the exception. I personally believe that our God is still a God of miracles. I've witnessed too many miracles not to believe that miracles are for today. We have entered the season of miracles. There will be major turnarounds in the lives of God's people as well as businesses, countries and economies. I declare it again, EXPECT THE UNEXPECTED!

God is going to turn around impossible situations, and miracles will be the direct result. God's people who are in the know are presently realigning themselves for the greatest times of miracles known to this generation. We have our very own private appointed season, as God breaks into the natural course of things and turns around, through His Church, the atrocities of the enemy. He's letting the world know that Hell will not prevail against His church!

This season of expecting the unexpected must saturate every fiber of our beings. We have entered into the season of unexpected miracles. I recall days gone by when the church believed God could do anything, and, for the most part, He did. Doctors were not the first people we' would seek and make an appointment with when we were sick. Mom and Dad would bring us to church and to the altar and have the audacity to believe God was the Healer! He was and He did! We knew nothing about *moed*; all we knew was that faith in God worked.

In apologetics, I learned that a subjective experience could not be argued or disproved. I have seen too many miracles to turn back now. God miraculously healed my body from death's door at least twice that I remember and kept me from an early death a number of times.

When I was a child, my appendix ruptured, and doctors gave me only a fifty percent chance of survival.

Second, I had infected stomach tissue that resulted in gangrene within my stomach and intestines. According to the report of the surgeon, I had only six hours to live. I am thankful for the physicians and surgeons who took care of me, but both acknowledged that it was God who performed the miracle, not they themselves.

Are you willing to enter the season to allow God to manifest His greatness in your life? Is there a bad report concerning your health? Has everyone given up on you? Well, God hasn't, and He never will. The Scriptures declare that God *"does cures."* The implications of that word *cures* speaks of healing every type of sickness, disease and infirmity, both known and unknown. He is the Healer of every infirmity before it is even discovered by medical science.

DIVINE REVERSALS

I believe in divine reversals. I love divine reversals. I love it when the enemy of our souls believes he has us exactly where he wants us, and God "suddenly" turns his plots back on his head!

This is a season of divine reversals!

You need to grasp this in your spirit. Whatever the enemy has been plotting against you, there's divine reversal for you! Whatever you may be facing that is contrary to the Word of God, encourage yourself with His Word, and get ready for a turnaround! Expect the unexpected in the areas of your life that you are facing, lay hold of God and His Word, and watch the turnaround take place.

We're going to examine a few scriptures where a divine turnaround took place and grow in the faith of God to agree with and allow these turnarounds to happen for us today. In Nehemiah 13:2, it says: *"God turned the curse into a blessing." The Knox Translation* says, *"...only our God transformed that curse into a blessing."*

This is the story of Balak, King of the Moabites (enemies of God and His people) and Balaam (the prophet of God). Balak had seen that God's people had defeated the Amorites and that they were fearful of Israel. He, therefore, sent out messengers to Balaam for him to curse God's people so that Moab could become more in number and stronger than Israel.

Balaam sought the Lord concerning this matter and, of course, God told him he could not curse His people. God said to Balaam, *"You shall not curse the people: for they are blessed"* (Numbers 22:12, NKJV).

There are numerous Scriptures throughout the Bible that declare that we are blessed and that we are blessed of the Lord. The enemy of your soul would try to convince you that you are cursed, that you are an outcasts and that God is not for you. Beloved, God is for you and since He is for you, "who can be against [you]?" (Romans 8:31). You cannot be cursed for God has blessed you!

Nehemiah said, *"God turned the curse into a blessing."* According to *Strong's Exhaustive Concordance of the Bible,* the word *turned* is from the Hebrew *hapak* and is defined as "to overturn, to turn around, to transform and reverse." God overturns curses, turns them around, transforms them and reverses them! God turns curses into blessings!

Notice, the enemy cannot reverse the blessing, but God can reverse the curse!

The enemy cannot reverse the blessing, but God can reverse the curse!

First Samuel 10:6 speaks of Saul and says, *"The Spirit of the Lord will come upon thee, and you will prophesy with them, and you will be turned into another man." The Knox Translation* says, *"...turning you into a new man."* Isn't that what God has done for us, turned us into another man? We are new creations in Christ with a heart after God and God's heart within us.

Saul was turned into another man. Again the word *turned* is from *hapak* and speaks of transforming man into a new creation. It also speaks of "turning around, overturning and reversing." God wants to turn our old man into a new man with a new heart. He wants to turn us around for His glory.

GOD REVERSED A SITUATION

Esther 9:1-4 reveals another instance in which God reversed a situation. In this case, He reversed the plans of the enemy to destroy His people. John 10:10 states emphatically what the plans of the enemy are for our lives: to steal, kill and destroy. *The Modern English Version* states, *"The thief never comes except to ... ."* The thief only shows up in life to destroy. If you are encountering the enemy, know this:

he's out for no good! But God reverses the schemes of the enemy and gives us life and life more abundantly.

The Beck Translation says, *"...and have it overflowing in them." The Moffatt Translation* says, *"...and have it to the full."* That's the God kind of life that He has for us through His Son Jesus.

Now, back to Esther. On the very day that the enemies of the Jews were going to carry out the decree of their execution, God turned it around for His people. Imagine living with a death sentence on your head for that period of time. Were they fearful? Were they running to hide? No! God had turned the plot of Haman back on him, and he was hung on the very gallows he had built to hang Mordecai (Esther's cousin). It may seem to some that God delays His deliverances, but the fact is that He is always on time, or should we say, in season.

Delay is not denial in God's economy!

Not only is God turning around the situations in your life; He is also bringing to nothing the plans of the enemy, as well as the enemy himself. Our enemy is already a defeated foe, and the very scheme he devises against us God turns back on him!

The NIV states it like this, *"the tables were turned and the Jews got the upper hand..."*

The Psalmist stated in Psalm 30:11, *"Thou hast turned my mourning into dancing for me."* The *Berkley Version* says it like this, *"Thou hast turned my lamenting into a processional."* Lamenting, of course, is an expression of grief, sorrow or regret. It's a very strong word describing the condition of one who has lost something or someone very precious and valuable.

A processional is :a musical composition designed for a continuous forward movement." I liken the lamenting with the loss of a loved one, for it is a great loss. It describes the deepest cry of one's heart because of death. But God has designed for us a divine reversal, a one hundred and eighty degree turnaround from deep despair to exuberant dancing on the streets! He puts a song in our hearts and a dance in our steps, and we are suddenly moving forward with life because of the divine reversal. God has overturned the sting of death; He has reversed our course, turned us around and set us on a forward motion.

The prophet Isaiah said that God has appointed *"unto them that mourn in Zion, to give unto them beauty for ashes, the oil of joy for mourning, the garment of praise for the spirit of heaviness"* (Isaiah 61:3). We have a divine appointment with Him, so that we *"might be called the trees of righteousness, the planting of the Lord, that he might be glorified!"* (same verse). This is another *moed* in our lives that we do not want to miss. This is the season for our turnaround over mourning!

Examine Psalm 35:4. It *"Let them be confounded and put to shame that seek after my soul: let them be turned back and brought to confusion that devise my hurt." The Harrison Translation* states it like this, *"May those who wish to kill me be dishonored and humiliated, may those who plan evil against me be routed and disgraced."* Sadly, these verses not only speak of the devil (who is the initiator of all that is evil and not good); it also speaks of people who are filled with evil. The psalmist called upon God to plead his case against his enemies.

I do not believe David enjoyed the destruction of his enemies. He simply wanted his safety. But when his enemies failed to respond, he had no alternative but to call on God for vindication. In this life, not everyone will be our friends or even like us for that matter.

We do not wish harm or evil upon anyone, but the consequences of those who harbor ill will against God's people have been determined by their own decisions to come against us. They will be dishonored or treated in a degrading manner (brought into low esteem) and humiliated (reduced to a lower position in one's own eyes or other's eyes; extremely destructive to one's self-respect). What a terrible situation to be in when one can feel so low that it becomes destructive to them.

Then it states that they will be routed (demoralized, to defeat decisively or disastrously) and disgraced (to cause to lose favor or standing, to humiliate by a superior showing). Disgrace is the condition of suffering loss of esteem and of enduring reproach, and it implies complete humiliation and sometimes ostracism (banishment). This is what was meant when God said He would turn them back. God brings complete loss to those who seek to destroy His own.

The definitions of the words we have used thus far, including and especially the word *turned,* were derived from *Strong's Exhaustive Concordance of the Bible.* I want to give just a brief history about Dr. James Strong so that we can see the providence of God that was at work for us long before we were ever born. Then I will show you what I believe to be one of the most monumental signs (*moed,* appointed signs) for us today.

Dr. James Strong, born in 1822, was a professor of exegetical theology at Drew University Seminary from 1868 to 1893. One year following his leaving the seminary, Dr. Strong passed away. But during his quarter century at Drew, his most important publication, *The Exhaustive Concordance of the Bible* was written (by hand) and published in 1894, the year of his death. To say that this man greatly impacted our understanding of the Bible would be a gross understatement.

I believe Dr. Strong was a prophetic seer for generations to come!

Rapidly approaching my fiftieth year of ministry, I have had a *Strong's Concordance* in my library and used it, alongside my Bible, more times than I can even count. It has saved me many times over in defining words and phrases used in the Bible. It is quite possible that if Paul would have had *Strong's Concordance* back in his day, it would have been that which he was referring to when he told Timothy that on his return from Troas to bring his "books" and especially his "parchments." Just a thought).

My reason for this information is to show you the providence of God and how He is showing us that we have entered a season of turnaround where we can expect the unexpected. Let me state this emphatically to you: I do not believe in coincidences. I believe in the Providence of God (defined by *Webster's* as "the power of God to divinely guide and sustain human destiny")!

A Season of Turnaround

Each example of the word *turned* used in this chapter and other chapters as well, as I said, is from the Hebrew word *hapak*" and means "to overturn, to turn around, to transform and reverse." In and of itself, I say that's pretty awesome. Wouldn't you agree? But here is the monumental sign (the *moed*). When you look up the word *turned* in *Strong's Concordance*, the reference number is 2015! The number 15 in the Bible is linked to victory over the enemy and a bountiful harvest! We have lived through the year 2015, and I believe that year was the beginning of the greatest turnaround the Church has ever experienced. "Was that a coincidence?" you may ask. Not if you believe in a God who knows the end from the beginning and can use a man 126 years before the date of this writing to pen prophetically for a generation of men and women of God who are looking for and are aligning themselves with His Word to experience a divine turnaround!

Think about that! 126 years ago God instructed a man to write prophetically for a future generation, a generation in which there would be men and women of God who refused to be silent and would declare His providence for the Church. I do not know if anyone else has gotten this revelation, but since I have, I must let as many people know as are within the scope of my ministry that God declared 2015 as the beginning of a tremendous season of turnaround. I refuse not to declare it! I have no shame in saying it.

"I have the right to remain silent, but I don't have the ability!" — Ron White

---

I expect the unexpected in this season of turn-around, and God has confirmed His Word to me with personal, private signs!

Chapter 4

A SEASON OF DOUBLES

"First seek to understand and then be understood."   — St. Francis of Assisi

In the economy of God you never get back the same amount you have invested. It's never dollar for dollar. Here's a revelation, "When you consider the principle of restoration, you'll see that God instituted the seedtime and harvest time as a clear indication and description of what He means when He speaks of restoration." Understanding that restoration means something that has been given, has been lost or stolen, and is now restored or brought back to the individual, we can definitely understand that God always has our best interests in mind.

Restoration means to get back greater in quality, quantity and deed.

Therefore, if something has been given, stolen or lost, God has your back! When you give to Him, you are doing it with a conscious effort. Therefore, God assures you that the principles of harvest and restoration are enacted on your behalf. Luke 6:38 specifically states, *"Give* [seed time], *and it shall be given unto you* [harvest time]; *good measure, pressed down, and shaken together, and running over, shall men give into your bosom* [restoration]. *"*

WOW! Can you grasp that? Do you see what God has provided for you through the principle of restoration, as well as seedtime and harvest time? You need to know that the power of one word from God can totally disrupt the lack you may be facing right now in your life. His rhema created galaxies and universes, and worlds without end. It can certainly change the course of your life today.

Some may say, "What if I'm not experiencing lack or trouble in my life?" I'm saying to you, AWESOME! But that doesn't mean you don't have to get more. In fact, the more you have and the more can you give to the Kingdom of God, the more He'll see to it that you'll have much more to extend His Kingdom on this Earth.

The power of His Word and glory are a present reality in the NOW of human life!

Don't put it off for some distant time or generation; *"Now faith is..."*

Let's examine the Law of Restitution for a moment. The Law of Restitution will have a greater significance in this season of doubles, as God elevates His own. *Restitution* can be defined as "to give back to the rightful owner." But you need to remember that it's never dollar for dollar.

Exodus 22:4, 7 and 9 speak to the amount of restitution that was to be paid back because of a wrongful deed done against someone. Verses 3, 5, 6, and 12 each use the word *restitution*. The Scriptures declare that the restitution that was to be paid back was double!

Listen, the enemy cannot steal from you without having to recompense you for what's been stolen. There's an admonition that is given to you today to call back, with a double portion, those things that have been robbed from you in past years. This is a season of restoration and restitution. Double restitution will manifest in your life as you appropriate the Word to your situation.

Another scripture I want to bring to your attention is found in Job 42:10. In case you're not familiar with the book of Job, I'd first like to rehearse his story for clarification.

Job was the wealthiest man of his day. He, according to the testimony of God, was a man of integrity and maturity who loved God and rejected evil. In fact, God went as far as to say that there was none like Job in all the earth. It's pretty awesome for God to give that kind of character reference about someone. But let's see what transpired in this man's life as the enemy attacked him and stole all he had.

First, Job 1:14 it states that his oxen were plowing and his donkeys feeding beside them, and the enemy took them and killed his servants. As I said earlier, Job was the wealthiest man of his time. This verse speaks to his agricultural business, which we understand. But have you ever considered that it may hold many more implications as well?

The oxen were not only used to plow fields, but they were also used in sacrifice (offer) to God. Sacrifice was related to worship. Therefore the enemy, first of all, stole Job's ability to offer up a sacrifice to God in worship. This is always the first tactic of the enemy, to rob you of your ability to worship, whether it's through discouragement, disappointment or dealing with daily life, and not offer to God the worship which rightly belongs to Him alone.

Again, in Job 1:16, the enemy caused fire to fall from heaven, and it destroyed Job's sheep.

This speaks about Job's meat production. Then, in verse 17, it says that the enemy came and stole his camels. This speaks of Job's ability to transport his goods (modern-day travel trailers, if you will).

Finally, verse 19 describes the enemy taking (killing) Job's sons. What a devastation this man experienced—and all because of his character toward God. May I say to you that the enemy is not really after you; he's after the God testimony in your life.

But look at the response of this man of God found in Job 1:20-22. Losing all you have is bad enough (you can start afresh and rebuild). But losing your sons ... , now that's a different set of circumstances. (I know what I'm talking about, I lost a son). Still, in this, the greatest crisis of his life, Job arose and worshipped God! Although the enemy seemingly stole his ability to offer up to God in sacrifice, the man picked himself up and worshiped His Creator! The Scriptures say that he *"blessed ... the name of the Lord!"* (verse 21).

When all was said and done, the Scriptures declare, *"In all this Job sinned not nor charged God foolishly"* (verse 22).

This is the backdrop, the foundation the man began with, which ultimately leads us to Job 42:10. Not only did God heal Job of his sicknesses (*"The LORD turned the captivity of Job"*); it says that the Lord gave Job double what he had before! God always restores greater in quality, quantity and deed!

Have you considered Proverbs 6:31, where it declares that if an enemy steals from you and he is found, *"he shall restore sevenfold!"* That's greater than double, isn't it? Look at the remainder of that verse where it says, *"he shall give all the substance of his house."*

Preachers, this is the season where we boldly proclaim to our congregations what the Word says concerning restoration and restitution. People of God, it's the season to reap what you have sown, what has been stolen or what has been lost. We have the authority to plunder the entire enemy's camp. We just didn't know it until now!

Let's examine Zechariah 9:9-12. In this text God is exhorting Zion to rejoice for the coming Messiah and is defending His Church.

God says that He will bring deliverance to His people (His Church) and declares, *"Turn to the strong hold, ye prisoners of hope"* (verse 12).

I was raised with the understanding that a stronghold was a bad thing. You can't listen to many ministries today without them speaking of demonic strongholds. In fact, it's almost as if those strongholds are somehow greater than God. I don't deny that these strongholds exist. In fact, Paul was very explicit in declaring to the church at Corinth that God's weapons are mighty in pulling down strongholds of the enemy that exist in our minds. But there is a stronghold that is virtually never mentioned, and this stronghold is the one we should be speaking about and declaring. This stronghold lives within us.

This verse describes God as a stronghold! Now that's a stronghold I can live with and the One I refuse to live without! He's greater than any stronghold the enemy may attempt to imprison you with. Make God your Stronghold, and every situation in your life will have to bow to Him.

A Season of Doubles

I live by faith and am bound by hope and rely solely upon my stronghold—my God! This is the formula in which God says He will render (to transmit to another, deliver, give up to, yield) to those who are His prisoners of hope and who turn to Him, double!

I would be remiss if I stopped here and did not speak of the blood covenant. I want you to notice another feature of these verses. There is no guarantee greater in this life than the Word of God. No dealership, bank, or any manufacturer can give you a better guarantee, or even come close to the written guarantee of the Word of God. We have assurance through the blood covenant that what God says will come to pass.

We stand eternally grateful for the redeeming blood of Jesus that was shed for us that we might be freed from the grip of the enemy. And, although there's not that much being spoken these days concerning the power of the blood of Jesus, it still does not negate the fact that without the shedding of blood, there is no remission. God has made His covenant with His own through the blood of Jesus. He states that by the blood of the covenant He has released His own from dry and thirsty places, to bring them to Him to receive the benefits spoken of earlier. It is through the blood covenant that we have access to double in this life.

There's a scripture that has been misquoted over the years by well-meaning people. Hebrews 9:22 quoted to say, "...without the shedding of blood, there is no remission of sin." This is a true statement and can be proven elsewhere throughout Scriptures, but that's not what the writer to the Hebrews was saying. He said, *"Without the shedding of blood is no remission."* He stopped at the word *remission*.

Remission is a medical term meaning that someone has a disease, but it's no longer active. It's gone dormant. For example, shingles is a chicken pox virus that is dormant in the nerve endings and can become active at any time. Even if it is not active, it may still be there. Doctors will say about a cancer that is under control "It is in remission." It may not be active, but it's still there and can once again become active. I'm grateful that the blood goes beyond sin and can stop other components of the enemy in every area of our lives. The Greek word translated as *remission* is *aphesis* and means "a cancellation, a cessation, to stop." Hear me, the progression of the enemy's attacks upon our lives are halted and removed by the blood of the covenant!

In this season, you can expect the cancellation not only of sin, but of sickness, disease and poverty over your lives!

There's a restoration of healings and miracle release that will invade the Church as never before, as we look to our Stronghold and live within the blood covenant!

I want us to look at another revelation the Lord gave me many ears ago. It is even more relevant today than it was then. The Word of

God is perpetual (continual, forever, everlasting). Its application is from generation to generation. Over time, this Word has evolved within me to cause me to grow in the greatness of our God. I've learned much over the years, as I was instructed by many great men of God who would speak into my life through their teachings as well as their lives and experiences. One such man is a man I hold in the utmost esteem: Dr. Ronald Cottle.

I hold Dr. Ronald Cottle in the utmost esteem!

My wife and I had the distinct pleasure of attending Dr. Cottle's 80th birthday party/ dinner and an opportunity to spend some quality time with this giant of the faith. In the short time we had together, he deposited truths in our lives that have revolutionized our hearts and renewed our pursuit of God in ways that had gone dormant. (I didn't even realize they were dormant.) He spoke prophetically over me and Monique and told me that I have God's mantle upon my life. I knew that in theory and had I lived it realistically, but it was an awakening for me to hear it again. I always knew I had His mantle, but it was great to hear someone who hadn't known me acknowledge that the mantle of God was in my life.

I had long respected and learned so much from this man from afar, never before having the pleasure to meeting him personally. All of his writings and all his accomplishments do not even come close to who this man really is and what he really means to the Kingdom of God. He made the statement, "A true father awakens wealth within his son."

"A true father awakens wealth within his son!"
— Dr. Ronald Cottle

It was shortly after that when God spoke to me about the revelation of seasons.

This next chapter will deal with another revelation that was given to me many years ago, but is more relevant today than the day I received it from God. Embrace the truths, enjoy the revelations, expect the unexpected!

Chapter 5

A SIXTH-DAY BLESSING

"He is no fool who gives what he cannot keep to gain what he cannot lose." — Jim Elliot

According to our calendar, we are presently living in the seventh millennium after Christ's birth. Although this may differ somewhat from the Jewish calendar, we'll utilize our calendar for purpose of clarification and understanding. Either calendar we use, this truth stands true. A text that attracted my attention is found in Luke 13:31-32. It is a prophetic word that Jesus spoke concerning His day, the next day and the last day. Another scripture to add to our understanding of these days is found in 2 Peter 3:8. It states, *"Be not ignorant of this one thing, that one day is with the Lord as a thousand years and a thousand years as one day."* In grammar, this is what is called a simile. A simile is "a comparison using the words *like* or *as*." One interpretation of this verse speaks of a literal day with the Lord being a thousand years. If that is the case, then what Jesus spoke in His prophecy takes on special significance for us today.

Theologians have determined that from Adam to Jesus was four thousand years, or, using the simile, four days, with Jesus beginning the fifth millennium or the fifth day. With this in mind, now look at Jesus statement in Luke 13:32:

> *Behold ... I do cures to day* [His day or the fifth day] *and to morrow* [the sixth day], *and the third day I shall be perfected.*

The word *tomorrow* speaks about the next millennium or the sixth day. The phrase *third day*, or, as it is rendered in verse 33, *"the day following,"* speaks of the seventh day or the final millennium. Isn't that awesome?

A Double Portion

But let's examine a few other scriptures that will enhance our understanding about the season of doubles with relation to the prophetic words of Jesus.

Deuteronomy 21:15-17 denote the portion of an heir. According to the text, the portion of an heir was to be a double portion! The double portion was called *"the right of the firstborn."* "But what does that have to do with me today?" you might ask. I'm glad you asked! Let's examine Hebrews 12:22-23. I want to bring to your attention the fact that the word *church* was never used in the Old Testament. In the New Testament, what was called *believers* in the Old Testament were now called "the Church in the Wilderness," "body," "group," "nation," "a people" and "the called-out ones."

You will never find the word *church* used in the Old Testament. It is a distinctively New Testament word. Some Old Testament words may be defined as church, but the word itself is New Testament.

This may not seem relevant to you until you read verse 23, with its reference to the heir. This verse says that we are called *"to the general assembly and CHURCH OF THE FIRSTBORN!"* We are called the firstborn ones, and we can and should be enjoying the rights of the firstborn, which is a double portion according to Deuteronomy 21:15-17.

Now examine 2 Kings 2:1-14. This story is about the prophet Elijah and about Elisha, his servant and protege. Elisha had faithfully served and followed the prophet and was being personally taught by him. It appears that Elisha had been under the tutelage of Elijah at least ten years when this incident we're about to discuss took place. The significance of time is relevant in that it is vital for believers to link up with and lock arms with those who have been faithful and have experienced the glorious works of God.

You can tell me of your experience, but I would rather experience it with you. That's what Elisha had lived for the years he was with Elijah. He was not only taught; he saw and experience the greatness of God.

Look at Matthew 11:4. The text speaks of John the Baptist being imprisoned. He told two of his disciples to find go Jesus and ask Him if He was the one that should come or should they look for another Messiah? Look at Jesus' response to the two followers of John in verses 4-6. Jesus told them to go back to John and tell him what they had heard and seen.

The two disciples were taken on a special trip with Jesus and witnessed firsthand the blind receiving their sight, the crippled made to walk, the lepers cleansed, the deaf receiving their hearing, the dead being raised to life and the poor having the Gospel preached to them. Can you understand the implications of these verses? These men were eyewitnesses of the power of Jesus and were able to tell John, not only what they had heard, but also what they had seen.

I do not believe it's coincidental that Jesus' disciples were with Him when He performed miracles. It wouldn't be long before He would send them forth to do the same mighty works (see Luke 10).

sI recall hearing about the miraculous power of God before I personally experienced it. I would long for God to use me to heal, deliver, and see souls saved from eternal damnation.

There was a guest speaker whose name was Marvin Gorman!

One Tuesday evening in a church service, there was a guest speaker whose name was Marvin Gorman. That evening I learned many things about him. First of all, to my surprise, he was an accomplished guitarist. But more than that, he brought the Word of God to life as he ministered. He did more than preach what God would do; he demonstrated what God could do. Although I was only fourteen years young at the time, I determined that since God had already called me to minister His Word, I wanted to preach like Brother Gorman.

Not only did I want to preach like Marvin Gorman; I wanted God to use me like him in the miraculous. I began to study under him through cassettes (for the younger generation, that was our version of CDs) and attended meetings he held in my area. I witnessed firsthand the blind receiving their sight, deaf people hearing again, and the crippled walking and running around the church! Through Marvin Gorman's ministry, I saw hundreds filled with the baptism of the Holy Spirit.

I made it my business to learn all that I could through this man, and he became my spiritual father. He invested ministry in me, put vision in my spirit, made an eternal deposit within me and mentored me for the Kingdom's sake. I am still learning from him today through his CDs and books. I can truthfully say that if I had not been exposed to the actual power of God at work and had not personally witnessed His miracles, I sincerely question as to whether or not I would be used of God as I am today. I say without hesitation but with much humility of heart, that God uses me in the miraculous today. I have personally been used of God to heal the sick, open blinded eyes, watch the lame walk again, win souls for His Kingdom, set at liberty the captive, operate in the gifts of the Holy Spirit, receive revelation knowledge, and see multitudes filled with His glorious Holy Spirit.

I give God all the glory and am grateful for the day He put Rev. Marvin Gorman in my life!

I said all that to lead us to this point where Elijah asked Elisha what he could do for him before he was taken to Heaven. What was it that Elisha asked of Elijah when Elijah was about to be taken up? Elisha had been with Elijah all those years and had seen the power of God at work in his life, and he wanted what Elijah had! Elisha told him he wanted a double portion of his spirit. He asked for the portion of the heir, the double portion! He wanted what his father had!

Elijah told the younger man he had asked a hard thing, but if he saw him when he was taken, it would be done for him. Why would Elijah say it was a hard thing? Because if you will remember, the portion of the heir, a double portion, was reserved especially for the first born. In essence, Elisha was saying to Elijah, "Make me your firstborn son!" Elijah responded by telling Elisha that if he saw him taken away, his request would be granted.

The story continued. Elisha saw Elijah taken up and then he said something unusual, *"My father, my father, the chariot of Israel, and the horsemen thereof"* (2 Kings 2:12). "What is so unusual about that?" you may ask. In that culture, a servant was never allowed to address his master as father; that was reserved only for the firstborn son. When God took Elijah up and Elisha witnessed it, a transformation took place. Elisha was changed from being a slave to being the firstborn son of Elijah with all the rights of the firstborn! He received Daddy's portion!

Again you may ask, "What does that have to do with me?" I refer you to Galatians 4:4-7, which states: *"But when the fullness of the time was come, God sent forth his Son, made of a woman, made under the law, to redeem them that were under the law, that we might receive the adoption of sons. And because ye are sons, God has sent forth the Spirit of his Son into your hearts, crying, Abba, Father. Wherefore thou art no more a servant, but a son; and if a son, then an heir of God through Christ."* Can you see it? These verses tie together to state emphatically that we are the Church of the Firstborn and our right as the firstborn is a double portion! We are a sixth-day people and have been appointed by God to accomplish in our generation what has not been given to any another previous generation.

I am not addressing the entire millennium of the sixth-day people, for most have gone on, but the final generation of the millennium. We have done what few generations have done before us. We have bridged a gap between two millenniums! And we will do what no generation has ever done before—walk in the seasons of the Lord simultaneously so that in this day (the seventh day, the last millennium), He will be perfected!

I must ask, "How will He be perfected?" I believe it will be through a people who will demonstrate His purpose in their lives, people who will not be intimidated by the enemy, people whose lives reflect the character of Christ. It will be a people who will live in the demonstration of His power by enjoying the prosperity He alone can provide for us and going about showing His miraculous deeds. You, each of you reading this writing, are the candidates God has chosen to show forth His glory. It's your choice to enter into the seasons of suddenlies and discover your destiny, pursue it with a hot passion and enjoy what otherwise you could never have obtained.

Chapter 6

THE CREATIVE POWER OF GOD

"Inside every failure is a success struggling to get out. Your inner seed is your key to success." — Dr. Ronald Cottle

We have gleaned so much from history by examining the names and surnames of people. Everything from their hair color, to their occupations, where they resided and even their behavior has been discovered simply because of their names. It should be of no surprise to believers that the names of God identify who He is. The Bible is filled with the names of God, which describe His attributes and His character.

We will examine just a few that are probably not new to you, but it's necessary so that we can understand the remainder of the chapter.

The first name of God we want to review is the one found in Genesis 22:14—Jehovah-Jireh:

And Abraham called the name of that place Jehovahjireh: as it is said to this day, In the mount of the LORD it shall be seen.

The Holman Christian Standard Bible writes it: *"The LORD Will Provide ... . It will be provided on the LORD's mountain."* *The Bible Dictionary* defines Jehovah-Jireh as "the God who provides" and further adds that "in the mount of the Lord it shall be seen." This has been regarded as an equivalent to the saying, "Man's extremity is God's opportunity."

The *Septuagint* (Greek translation), gives the meaning as *"the Lord has seen."* The Jewish Translation includes, "in the mount where the Lord is seen." And *Strong's Concordance* further adds, "The Lord will see." These are all eye openers.

I want to take a little latitude as I discuss the basic meanings of Jehovah-Jireh. First of all, we know that His name declares that He is the God of provision. So often we limit our scope of understanding to the particular situation in which an event occurs.

We need to broaden our perspective, especially when it comes to God, and recognize that He is our total Provider!

I often see that one of God's attributes connects with many of His other attributes. It's as though there are crossovers from one characteristic to another. What is it that the Lord provides? I believe it depends, not only on the need you are currently facing, but to every aspect of your life—whether it be good or bad. Can you receive this?

Jehovah-Jireh provides blessings to the blessed, health to the healed, prosperity to the secured, and every other channel you may think. Also, to the hungry, He provides nourishment; to the weak, He provides strength; to the needy, He provides provision; to the hurting, He provides relief; to the sin-sick, He provides wholeness, and we have not even begun to touch the surface of what Jehovah-Jireh provides. His provision is as great as our needs and even beyond the needs we face. He's Jehovah-Jireh, the Lord our Provider!

Notice the mentality of Christians who associate God as Provider only when they are down and out and about to lose it all. No, my friend, God is bigger than just an answer to my need; He's Jehovah-Jireh!

Paul said to the Ephesian church that God is *"able to do exceeding abundantly above all that we ask or think, according to the power that worketh in us"* (Ephesians 3:20). This tells me there is nothing in Heaven or Earth or beyond that God is not the Provider for.

The next thought about Jehovah-Jireh is that the Lord sees the need before the need is manifested. Or, even greater than that, He has already provided the manifestation of provision before we face the need. I cannot help but believe that at the same time Abraham and Isaac were going up the mountain on one side, the ram to take Isaac's place was heading up the other side! This is what Jehovah-Jireh is all about! The Scriptures declare that He sees the end from the beginning, and since that is the case, God has already made provision for you even before the need appears! Our answers are there even before the question is asked. If you can grasp that, then you will know that the enemy of your soul can never get the upper hand on you. Listen to this, rehearse it over and over in your soul and declare it with your mouth: "I have no successful enemies!"

I have no successful enemies!

That's right! Because of Jehovah-Jireh, we have no successful enemies! So the One who sees and has seen is the One who is your Provider.

The next name we want to discuss is also a favorite, as well as a familiar one, with many

Christians—Jehovah-Rapha. This particular name of God means, "the Lord our Healer." Exodus 15:26 states, *"I Am the LORD that healeth thee."* Young's Literal Translation says it this way: *"For I, Jehovah, am healing thee."* A translation of the Old Testament Scriptures from the Original Hebrew states, *"For I am Jehovah, thy physician."* The Knox translation states, *"I am the LORD, and it is health I bring thee."* The Bible: an American Translation interprets it this way, *"For I, the LORD, make you immune to them."*

I purposely used more translations to define Jehovah-Rapha than I did with Jehovah-Jireh because people today are more inclined to believe in a God who can or will provide, but have more difficulty believing in a God who heals. I want to also inject that these two names of God will fit perfectly with the last name of God that we'll discuss shortly.

I imagine there are various reasons why some believe that God can, but doesn't perform miracles any longer. The subject of a God who heals today has been the subject of many discussions over the centuries—our day included. I have personally read writers who have adamantly declared that to believe God heals today is equivalent to blasphemy. Others have denied His involvement with man altogether (the deists). Still others say they believe God can, but proceed to let you know why He will not heal. My purpose in this subject is not necessarily to inform you of those who do not believe that God heals, but to show you, by His very nature and name, that He most certainly does.

Medical advances over the past century have been mind-boggling. Cures have been found for various diseases and sicknesses that before were a sentence of death. Research continues today to address and hopefully conquer many diseases that fill our world. Multiplied billions of dollars are spent each year for these studies. Understand that this author is not against physicians, discoveries, medical science or any other avenue that stands to eliminate maladies. Of course, with all this research and the billions that are invested in these studies, there is still no guarantee that healing will be realized.

Nonetheless, I stand with them in their attempt to bring healing to the sick. I do believe that they—the scientists, medical personnel, etc.—are God-given gifts to us who are enabled by Him to work hand in hand with Him for the betterment of our society. The sick need a physician. And no, this is not contradictory. Nor do I support those who advocate that God no longer heals.

"Lord, I believe; help thou my unbelief" (Mark (:24) was the statement made by the father of a deaf and dumb child Jesus delivered. Faith must grow.

Faith grows between the times you think God has to answer and the time when He finally does answer!

With all of that said, why is it that man refuses to believe in and accept a direct statement made by God Himself who describes Himself as "The Lord Who Heals?" Has mankind been so bombarded, so brainwashed to the point that we trust men more than God? Has religion so filled the hearts of people that they would rather put their trust in religious bondage than in God? "Is it easier to believe that God can, but I'm not sure He will or that He'd do it for me?" These are questions you must answer for yourself. Herein lies the choice you must make: God or man? Has our preaching become so diluted that faith is not generated in the hearers? Have we not witnessed any healings that show and prove that God still heals? Jesus went about preaching and showing the Good News of the Kingdom of God (see Luke 8:1). You have probably heard it before and possibly read it somewhere before, but it bears repeating: "Where do you find in the Word of the Eternal God that healings and the miraculous have ended?"

Where do you find in the Word of the Eternal God that healings and the miraculous have ended?

Quite the contrary, history is filled with testimonies of the miracles and healings of God in His people and in unbelievers as well! That our God is a healing God cannot be disputed or denied. This author has not only been a recipient of God's miracles and healings, but I am used of God to bring healing to many in His Kingdom. Many are healed in our services, not only spiritually and emotionally, but physically as well. I make no attempt to answer why everyone is not healed, but I'll refute to the end any claim that our God is not Jehovah-Rapha! If only one person has received a healing or a miracle, then the teaching that God does not heal or perform any miracles any longer is wrong.

I refer you again to two translations of Exodus 15:26. First, the Knox Translation states, *"It is health I bring to you."* Notice what God is bringing to His people: health! Multitudes are due for a visitation from God (a *moed*) and He's bringing health to you! Get ready for your suddenly! Health is on the way and it's being hand-delivered by none other than God Himself! This is a season in time when you can receive healing for the sickness that has held you down for so long. Some of you may be sensing the healing anointing as you read this. I believe that because I sense the anointing as I'm being directed by God to write this. Reach out to the Healer and receive your health!

Expect the unexpected. Receive your healing and whatever else God wants to deliver to you in this season.

Secondly, The Bible: An American Translation, interprets Exodus 15:26 like this: *"For I, the Lord, make you immune to them."* Talk about a "WOW" factor!

This translation takes it even beyond the thought of healing to a God who makes us immune to sickness and disease!

Now that's foreign to our theological understanding. I mean, imagine being immune to
sickness. Sounds to me like God wants us to
be like He originally intended us to be, free of
sickness. I must confess to you that I believe
in the totality of the atonement; i.e. spirit, soul
and body. But to be immune from sickness ... ,
give God a people that believes His Word and
relies upon Him, and let's see what God will
do in this season of suddenlies.

Allow me to inject this one thought before we
continue: What about the Church becoming a
House of Healing?

What about the Church becoming a House of Healing?

Humor me. Please read 1 Chronicles 4:12.
In that verse, you'll find the name Beth-Rapha.
Abrarium Publications' Theological Dictionary
defines this name as a "village in the territory
of Judah of which Eshton was the father, which
means either the founder or the chief at the

time of the writing." The word *beth* means "house" in Hebrew, and we have just discovered the meaning of *rapha*. If you put these two words together you have *Beth-Rapha* or the "House of Healing!" The village was named The House of Healing! Why not allow God's House to be the House of Healing?

Let's allow God to save, to provide, to comfort, to give beauty for ashes, the oil of joy for mourning, a garment of praise for the spirit of heaviness, and let Him restore healing back to His House! That will glorify His name.

The final name of God I want us to look at in this chapter is found in Genesis 1:1, where it states, *"In the beginning God created the heavens and the earth."* The Hebrew name for God in this verse is *Elohim*, meaning My Creator. Again, I want to say that the names of God interweave with each other and crossover with each characteristic and attribute of God. You cannot separate the nature of God from His character any more than you can separate His attributes from Him.

He has declared, *"I am God, I change not."* God is eternal—past, present and future—the same yesterday, today and forever. He is Alpha and Omega, the One who was and is and is to come. Plainly stated, whatever He was, He is and He always will be.

Elohim is formed from *El*, Hebrew for "God, mighty One, strong." Whenever *im* is added to *El* in the Bible it indicates plurality. That's one reason why Jesus could say in John 1:1, *"In the beginning was the Word and the Word was with God and the Word was God."* In Colossians 1:15-20, Paul stated concerning Christ that He, Jesus, is *"the image of the invisible God, the firstborn of every creature. ... all things were created by him, and for him"* (verses 16). My purpose in describing the character and attributes of God in Genesis is to show you something about our Creator that may be new to some and maybe not to others.

Allow me to ask you this question, "When did God stop being a Creator?" Some will say, "Following the creation of earth or the galaxies" or whatever their concept of Heaven and Earth is. Others will honestly say that they don't know, while others mentally assent to the fact that He is Creator, but refuse to go any further than that. It is alien to our thinking that Elohim is *still* the Creator. Again, many factors contribute to this thinking, including religious beliefs, lack of teaching, poor preaching and the list goes on. But let me cut to the chase and tell you that God is still the Creator, and He's still creating today! You cannot strip God of His glory, He's the Creator.

What He WAS, He IS, and what He IS, He ALWAYS WILL BE!

Let me show you something in Isaiah 48 that the Lord spoke to my heart about. The background to this text is God showing His people how obstinate they had been. God told them in verse 3 that He had declared (prophesied) what would happen, and He spoke (prophesied) out of His mouth and He showed them, and He (God) did them suddenly, and they came to pass. God told them before it came to pass, The reason He spoke it first before it happened was that He didn't want His people to say their own hands had performed it, or an idol they had been worshipping had performed it, or they already knew it. God wanted His people to know that they had a Creator in their midst who could still create for their good. So He let them know what He was going to create before He created it.

The scripture then says in verse 6, *"You heard it, you see all this and will you still not declare it."* This is where I come in and any other person who fears not to declare the entire counsel of God. I'm declaring that God is still the Creator! I have heard Him speak prophetically in meetings, He has spoken prophetically to me personally, I have spoken prophetically to others and watched His Words come to pass, and now I must declare, prophesy, to you that Jehovah is still our Creator. We, the Church, must become a loud voice to our world, declaring the attributes and character of our God! We cannot be silent any longer because God insists that we declare His doings. This is the season in which we'll experience God creating for us ways that lead us into depths and regions beyond where we have ever gone before. Creative miracles, creative healings, and creative provisions will come because God is still creating! God says that "suddenly" He'll do them, and they'll come to pass!

Finally, examine verse 7 and get ready to be blessed! The New English Bible translates this verse as saying, *"They were not created long ago, but in this very hour."* The Jerusalem Bible states it like this, *"They created just now, this very moment."* Can you grasp what the Word, the Creator, has just spoken to you? God is saying that He will create in the very moment of your situation, a way of escape. He is saying that to prove to you that He's God. He is Creator. He will. in the very hour of your dilemma, create for you what you need. And it's going to be in a way you've not known before.

Too often we feel that we have God figured out. We know how He is going to move. We know how He's going to bless or lead us out of a predicament, or how He's going to manifest whatever it is we need. "He did it this way before." But God says, "No, you're not going to be able to say you knew it." EXPECT THE UNEXPECTED!

If God is going to do that for the obstinate, how much more will He do it for those who choose to follow Him in obedience and walk the life of faith? Allow your Creator, in this season, to speak (prophesy) to your situation and watch Him create the stage for His Word to come to pass. God will never leave Himself without a witness. And you and I are becoming His witnesses for this season!

Allow me to close this chapter by stating three important truths we must understand:

First, God speaks to people He's visiting. If you're reading this book, get ready for the visitation of your life. Open your heart to Him and receive His coming to you.

Second, God speaks to our potential and purpose. Since you're reading this book, allow God to maximize His potential to fulfill the purpose He has designed for you.

Thirdly, God will speak (prophesy) to specifics more than generalities. Now follow His prophetic words to your destiny, His specific design for your life.

Chapter 7

A Seed Plot Prosperity

"In a time of universal deceit, telling the truth is a revolutionary act."

— George Orwell

I woke up on the morning of the May 18, 2015 and the thought of a seed plot was in my spirit. I pondered about that for a moment and realized that I knew about a food plot, but had never heard about a seed plot. Of course, logic would dictate that in order for there to be a food plot, it must begin with a seed plot. I began to contemplate the seed plot and it was revealed to me what I didn't know. And it's the revelation that followed that I want to share with you in this chapter.

Being from south Louisiana and being raised on a sugar cane plantation and familiar with sugar cane, I began relating the sugar cane crop with the seed plot thought I had received. With sugar cane, the harvest becomes your seeding for perpetual years.

For example, in farming sugar cane, every fourth year the crop becomes the seed cane. As long as you continue seeding, you'll continue having a harvest. If you ever stop seeding, you'll stop harvesting. But the plots are alternated so that you'll have a harvest every year and you are seeding every year. You are never without a harvest if you never stop seeding.

I call this calculated sowing and reaping. Every season has a seed time and a harvest time. I, by no means, intend to imply that you seed only once a year. In fact, the more you seed, the more you will harvest. Consider this: what would your life be if you would seed daily? It stands to reason that the time would come when you' would also harvest daily.

Every harvest is an opportunity to invest seed into your future!

The Lord spoke to my heart in the third week of May 2014 and said, "Your harvest is just a seed sown away." I believe in the scriptural principles of prosperity. There are many who advocate that God never intended His people to prosper or that the prosperity the Bible speaks about is spiritual. I agree with spiritual prosperity, but I also believe that the Word speaks of other prosperities as well.

For the most part, those who disagree that God wants His people to prosper financially usually are very prosperous themselves (at the expense of those they claim shouldn't prosper). They remind me of the Pharisees who refused to enter the Kingdom of God and didn't want anyone else to enter either (see Matthew 23:13). It is time that we take God at His Word and prove that He will open up Heaven and pour out blessings that we will not have room enough to receive. This will take a people of tenacity who will take nothing less than what God's Word says.

"I'm looking for a lot of men with an indefinite capacity for not knowing what can't be done!" — Henry Ford

---

Joel says that your *"vats will overflow with wine and oil"* (Joel 2:24). A vat is an extremely large container. Imagine a large container that does not have the capacity to contain the harvest. I'm talking about a container built to hold an entire harvest. Yet God said that the instrument created to hold the harvest will be too small. Malachi 3:10 states that if we honor God with our tithe and offerings, He'll *"open you the windows of heaven and pour you out a blessing, that there shall not be room enough to receive it."* Hear me, God wants to flood you (the container made to embrace the harvest), in such a way that you'll overflow with His blessings! The oil and the wine are restoring qualities of the Lord. The entire text of Joel 2:18-32 speaks of the restoration of what has been stolen, destroyed or delayed, and God is restoring it all!

"What's the holdup?" you may ask. I would say that, for the most part, the holdup is that God's people are not aware of the season we've entered and the principles that God has laid out in His Word. It is also possible that we have been diluted with untruths to the extent that many do not believe that prosperity is possible for them.

The principles of God describe the way a promise is fulfilled. That's one reason for this writing. I want every child of God to be blessed and prosperous beyond their wildest expectation. In fact, I'll venture to say that some are so numb by the foolishness of error that even if blessings met them head on they'd refuse them. But I digress.

Twice in the book of Joel, verses 26 and 27, a statement is made that we must properly interpret if we' are to understand why we have been held up from the blessing. At the end of each verse it states: *"My people shall never be ashamed."* This word *ashamed* is from the Hebrew word *bos* and is defined as "to be delayed." We're waiting on God to do what He has already ordained He would do, while He's waiting for a people that will engage His Word and enter into a dimension that knows no delay! Look, He says in His Word that we should eat in plenty, be satisfied, and praise Him for His goodness in that He has dealt wondrously (to be marveled at). Know intimately that He is our God and will be never be delayed!

Amos 9:13 says that *"the days come, says the* LORD..." There's a day still to come. That day has not yet arrived, but it's coming. Are you ready for that day? Are you preparing for that day? Or will you concede to the doubters that the day is for everyone else and not for you? I submit to you that one of the days that Amos was prophesying about is a season of prosperity.

The scripture indicates that there will be days (more than one day) or seasons of prosperity.

Next, it says that the plowman will overtake

the reaper. Do you recognize the significance of that statement? The reapers are gathering the harvest as the plowman is breaking up the soil to sow seed for the next harvest. A plowman is a husbandman, a farmer. The husbandman and plowman are one and the same! He/she is the sower and the reaper! In other words, the days/ seasons are coming when your harvest catches up with your sowing, and they overlap each other.

Deuteronomy 28:2 says the blessings of the Lord "*will come upon us and overtake us.*" The word *overtake* in the Hebrew means "to catch up!" Imagine that, your reaping catches up with your sowing. It also means "to be able to afford." Some may say, "I give my tithe and an offering every paycheck, and that's the best I can do." God wants you in a position where you can afford to do better than that. If you purpose to sow toward a harvest that one day will overtake your sowing, and do it, the days will come that you'll be able to afford to do it. And you'll be able to afford it because you have done it and are doing it. The text says that the sower will overtake the reaper. Your seeding will surpass your reaping, and your reaping will surpass your sowing! Sounds to me like you'll be able to afford it. The more you sow, the more you'll reap! Sow every day for the season to come in which you will reap every day.

The remainder of Amos 9:13 says that the treader of grapes *"will overtake the sower of seed;* [there's that word overtake again} *and the mountains shall drop sweet wine and the hills shall melt."* The bottom line to this scripture is that plenty has been promised to those who sow seed and the harvest and the sowing will overlap.

If you will re-read the last three paragraphs and make notes on the revelations of His Word and meditate on those revelations, then make a decision to be one of His own who will not only say you believe His Word, but do it, then you'll see God do what He says He'll do for you.

Some will say, "It's too much of a sacrifice for me." I must ask, at this point, "Where is the sacrifice when God promises that you'll be able to afford it or that your income will catch up with your sowing? It ceases to be a sacrifice, and it becomes a pleasure and an opportunity to sow into God's Kingdom.

This is the seed plot we wrote about at the beginning of this chapter. The farmer/plowman/husbandman has seen to it, through the years, that he would never be without a harvest. He just keeps seeding and keeps harvesting at the same time and season. That's right, he seeds and harvests in the same season! We need to learn how to seed into our own harvest!

Here's a key principle: Just as the harvest never comes before the sowing, the blessings of the Lord never come before the seed. We have entered a season of supernatural increase. God is not only Jehovah-Jireh (God our Provider), He's also El-Shaddai, the God to whom nothing and no one is impossible, the God of More than enough, the God of the overflowing cup, the Almighty God and the God of Multiplication!

In the first week of May, 2014, God spoke to my heart and said, "When you take the limits off of Me, I'll bless you without limits." Imagine this: an entire field of money is yours for the taking. Would you casually just enter the field and pick here and there haphazardly? Or would you be passionate about getting in all the cash that's in that field? Passion can be defined as "caution set aside." We may all enter that field as a child who hunts eggs at Easter time, running here and there without any direction because of the excitement of all those eggs in the field. But the time would come when you would see to it that nothing would be left in the field. If you want to reap with a passion, you must first sow with a passion. Set caution aside when it comes to your sowing in order that you can harvest the abundance of your seed sown. Limitations are removed and supernatural provision is upon us! There is an influx of abundance in this season! This is your season of much more!

There are so many scriptures that speak to us that God wants us prosperous. Yes, in our spirit; yes, in our soul; yes, in our bodies; but also financially.

I remember a time when I was too poor to window shop. I would look in a store or a place of business, but I would not linger long because the pain of wanting something but not being able to get it would get to me. But not anymore. My God supplies and blesses without measure.

In the early part of 2015, Monique and I were ministering in Texas. While we were there, a minister from another church called me and said God had told him to bless us with a financial gift. He forwarded us the money. We blessed the Kingdom of God (giving the tithe and sowing a seed offering) and were extremely grateful that God still has people He can speak to that will hear and be obedient to His voice. When we arrived home, we discovered that someone had broken into our home and stolen our new television set. For a brief (I emphasize brief) moment, we stood there questioning why this would happen to us while we were fulfilling God's call upon our lives to minister at other churches. While we were being obedient to God, the enemy came in to steal. But look at this: before the enemy stole from us, God had already provided for us through the minister who blessed us. In fact, he had given us enough money, not only to replace the stolen television, but enough to purchase three televisions at the price of the one stolen if we wanted to! Of course, all we bought was one, but that's not the point. The point is that God knows the end from the beginning and stands ready to honor His own. God had provided the solution before we even knew there was a problem. The enemy comes to steal but God comes to give life abundantly.

Read the story of Abraham in Genesis 22, then cross-reference that with Hebrews 11:17-19 and see how obedience to the will of God gives you a confidence that God (Jehovah-Jireh) provides before there's ever a need. Yes the ram was there, but even if Abraham would have sacrificed his son, he was convinced that God was able to raise him from the dead! I speak this by permission; I believe God looked upon Abraham and Isaac and said, "Abraham, since you did not withhold your son from me, I'll not withhold My Son from you!"

Chapter 8

A FINAL WORD

What a tremendous season we are entering into. I have a strong belief that God has "kept the best for last." I believe in the coming of the Lord to take His children home. I also believe we are living in the final days, as we see His coming rapidly approaching. The clash between light and darkness is inevitable, as it has always been in history. I make no predictions about when Jesus will return, I only state what the Word of God says—He is returning. So I encourage you to prepare yourself for the greatest events of your life on this planet.

First of all, the seasons of suddenlies, and second, the coming of the Lord. Many will say, "With all that's happening in the world, how can you be so optimistic?" I say that the light always shines brightest in the darkest time. We are the light of the world and are about to shine brighter than ever before!

I do not believe that we're looking for a core of people who will follow God's bidding about the seasons. We already have the core. It's been here for a long time now.

Believers around the world have been anxiously awaiting what God is doing. It's a matter of accepting it, believing it, living it and enjoying it. The battle may not be over, but the victory has been won! There may be those who argue over the blessings you are about to receive and have been receiving since this season has begun. Just continue living it out within the season and watch as they enter in with you one by one.

I trust that this writing has enlightened you and encouraged you and prompted you to enter and enjoy the *Seasons of Suddenlies*.

ABOUT THE AUTHOR

Born and raised on a sugar cane plantation in the small southern town of Lockport,
Louisiana, **Jerry Fitch** has gone on to be
used by God to minister to multitudes across
America and abroad. A true Cajun, Jerry began school at the age of seven unable to speak
English. He overcame that hindrance and ex-
celled. Then, at the tender age of fourteen, he
accepted Jesus Christ as his Lord and Savior,
was filled with the Holy Spirit months later,
and soon accepted the call to minister the
Gospel.

Now, after more than forty years of ministry,
it is said that Jerry Fitch's revelations are as
fresh as ever, with an ever-increasing anointing
accompanying the delivery, to produce God's
expected result. Over the years, he has ministered in campmeetings, conventions, ministers'
conferences, church growth seminars, radio
and television programs, marriage enrichment
seminars, revivals and other noted services,

all the while pastoring churches in Louisiana, Texas, Michigan and Florida. He has weathered the storms of life, persevered during the greatest of trials and has surmounted seemingly impossible situations, knowing that God is in control of his lie.

Currently the Fitches pastor The Baldwin Church in Baldwin, Louisiana. He also maintains an apostolic oversight of Destiny Church, a church he founded in Jacksonville, Florida.

AUTHOR CONTACT PAGE

On the Web:
http://jerryfitchministries.com/

E-mail:
decajun2@aol.com

Phone:
(337) 831-0536

Mail:
Jerry and Monique Fitch
4204 Eldridge Street
New Iberia, LA 70563

BOOKS BY JERRY FITCH

Seasons of Suddenlies

...and other revelations of God's times and seasons

by Dr. Jerry Fitch

Introduction by Dr. Jerry Edmon

Moving
through
a Season
of Grief

You have turned my mourning into joyful dancing.
You have taken away my clothes of mourning and clothed me with joy.
Psalm 30:11

Jerry Fitch

THE

FINAL CALL

ARE WE PRESENTLY
RECEIVING THE FINAL CALL
OF THE SPIRIT?

JERRY FITCH

COMMUNION

TRUTH
VS.
TRADITION

JERRY FITCH